TABLE OF CONTENT

1.

INTRODUCTION.

Greetings from the world of billionaires, where being successful turns into a way of life and a distinctive way of thinking. In this context, adopting a millionaire's mindset involves more than simply becoming wealthy; rather, it involves developing a specific way of thinking and behaving that opens doors to prosperity and abundance. The first step on the path to becoming a billionaire is adopting this mindset, which consists of having a strong sense of self-worth, constantly seeking personal development, and being prepared to take measured risks.We will examine the different elements of a millionaire's attitude throughout this investigation and discover how this change in viewpoint can result in profound

1

achievement in all spheres of life. So, let's dig into the millionaire's mindset together if you're prepared to realize your full potential, widen your horizons, and start along the road to financial independence.

Chapter One; The Idea Of A Millionaire Mentality.

It takes a great deal of vision, passion, and laborious effort. Remain calm and wise, and remember that every obstacle is a teaching opportunity. Confidence and financial independence are easily attained if your objectives are clear and you stay focused.

What distinguishes the normal entrepreneur's mind from that of a millionaire? Five essential layers comprise a business mind, in my opinion: self conscious, principles, prioritization, discipline, and presence. But we don't always give each one due attention. We frequently focus entirely on the superficial levels, like presence and discipline, while utterly ignoring the deeper ones, in my opinion. However, it's like trying to construct a home on sand when you work from the top down.

Fortunately, a six-figure attitude may be developed or improved without spending a million dollars. All you have to do is know how to interact with each layer and what it signifies.

- 1. Self conscious;

Being able to look at our own actions with objectivity is a sign of self-awareness. Toxic identities and systems of thinking reside here since self-awareness influences everything we do.

Millionaires possess the ability to see their own thought processes from an elevated perspective, identify their assets and liabilities, and forge an identity that enables them to be the kind of people who achieve great things.

Initially, self consciousness arises from recognizing how our minds function. Not criticizing or punishing oneself for any harmful or negative behaviors you identify is an essential part of that. Observe them without passing judgment. Identifying a pattern and breaking it is the first step towards making a change.

For developing this kind of consciousness, meditation is an effective technique. It's easy to see what distracting thoughts come up when the objective is to concentrate only on breathing or a calming sound.

- 2. Fundamentals

You establish your values by building upon self consciousness. Your business's values are generally derived from the "what" and "why" of what you do. Your beliefs will never be easy to find, much less easy to stick to, if you lack self consciousness. Success will follow from understanding who you are and why.

- 3 Setting priorities

The capacity to plan, schedule, and prioritize is a crucial component of the millionaire mindset, and I've seen a lot of entrepreneurs lose their way at this point. Some people can spend whole days working on tasks that ultimately don't matter. Even though they seem to be moving forward, they are merely going around in circles. The millionaire is aware that what matters should receive unwavering attention. Even if it's the only thing they do in a given day, it's the one that tips the odds in their favor.

- 4 Reliability

The skill areas that the organization possesses are the disciplines, such as project management, marketing, accounting, sales, and relationship with consumers. Many business owners believe that in order to achieve great success, they must be authorities in just one field. SeeHowever, I've found that millionaires are typically generalists. Even though they may not possess an expert's depth of knowledge, they are enough knowledgeable in each area to be able to perceive the organization as a whole. This enables individuals to exercise sound judgment while making decisions, such as when to consult an expert.

- 5 Procedure.

Many professions have contributed to the numerous processes that comprise a business. From each discipline, several techniques might emerge. Marketing is a discipline that produces various techniques such as direct mail, brand messaging, paid advertising, and others.

Process is only a means to an end, as everyone with a millionaire mindset understands. Even while processes are the way a firm runs, they could not produce the desired results for entrepreneurs if the underlying layers are not understood.

Experts in business frequently advise people to "start at the bottom" in order to succeed. It's true that developing the proper mindset is more important than getting out of the mail room. You'll be far on your way to becoming self-aware if you just take that initial step!

Chapter Two; What Distinguishes The Millionaire Mindset From the Average Mindset, According To Psychology?

Aside from their monetary resources, the wealthiest individuals globally appear to have one thing in common: their character.

Positive and negative emotion regulation is a strength of these individuals, and they generally exhibit lower levels of emotional reactivity to their environment.

While they don't usually react the way other people would, this can come across as frigid. They frequently have an outgoing, extroverted personality and are receptive to new experiences.

This contradicts the widely held belief that millionaires are withdrawn, reserved individuals.

These psychological traits were more prominent the wealthier one was, even among non-millionaires with substantial endowments.

But what unites millionaires is more than just emotional restraint and extroversion.

Lastly, their agreeableness tends to be low. This does not imply that they are inherently impolite. Rather, it just indicates that they are at ease with disagreement. They don't have to win people over in order to confront them.

Rich people's and middle-class people's mindsets differ greatly from one another. Rich people generally perceive life as an endless stream of chances and obstacles to grow and thrive, whereas the middle class frequently feels constrained by their existing circumstances.

Middle-class people could view their capabilities as fixed or limited, whereas wealthy people are more likely to think that they can develop their skills and abilities through practice and hard work. Because they have a growth mindset, wealthy people are able to rise to new heights, accept difficulties, and learn from their mistakes.

If they are establishing a new business, buying stocks, or purchasing real estate, wealthy people are frequently more at ease with taking measured risks. They're prepared to take risks that the middle class might shy away from out of prudence or fear because they know that risk can lead to possible gain. Wealthy individuals often perceive the world as abundant with resources and opportunity, whereas those of the middle class may believe that there isn't enough for everyone. Rich people can be more giving, understanding, and hopeful about the future when they have an abundant attitude.

Rich people have different habits and behaviors from middle class people in addition to having different mindsets. These are some common approaches to life and money that wealthy people take.

Being physically and mentally fit is important to wealthy people because they understand that it's essential to their success. To preserve their vigor, energy, and attention, they make investments in good food, workout regimens, and self-care routines. Whether it's through coaching, schooling, or personal development initiatives, wealthy people think it's important to invest in oneself. They are prepared to spend time, money, and energy developing their skills and expertise because they consider themselves to be their most valuable asset.

SNumerous kinds of income, including stocks, enterprises, rental properties, and royalties, are common among wealthy individuals. Recognizing that depending solely on one source of income can be hazardous and constricting, they aim to enhance their security and riches by spreading their sources of income.

Rich people often have a variety of sources of income, such as stocks, businesses, rental properties, and royalties. They distribute their sources of income because they understand that having only one source of income can be risky and restrictive and that doing so will increase their wealth and security.

Their value system for time is another key difference. Because time is a limited resource, those who are wealthy see it as their most valuable possession. They set priorities for their time by concentrating on tasks that support their objectives and core beliefs and assigning or outsourcing non-essential work. They also schedule time for hobbies, vacations, and spending quality time with loved ones because they understand how important it is to rest and recharge.

The wealthy also prioritize value over price, which sets them apart from the middle class. Although the middle class is more likely to be price conscious and seek out the least expensive choice, the rich recognize the significance of quality and longevity. They are prepared to spend money on goods and services that could be more expensive up front but end up being more valuable in the long run.

Let's sum up by saying that wealth and income are not the only factors that distinguish the rich from the middle class. Rather, independent of one's financial circumstances, they are shaped by a confluence of values, habits, and attitude that are accessible to everybody. We may generate wealth and create an abundant and fulfilling life by adopting a growth mindset, taking cautious risks, investing in ourselves, putting our health and fitness first, and concentrating on long-term goals.

Chapter Three; Gaining Financial Stability and Creating Wealth.

Increasing your education, knowledge, and necessary professional abilities will help you progress in your career. Understanding finance is also necessary to make a living. Additionally, living a healthy lifestyle and being in good health will free up more time for you to pursue opportunities for earning money. Financial sufficiency, as determined by each individual, is a better indicator of financial stability than riches. Building financial stability typically requires time, since one must accumulate sufficient assets for future needs and potential emergencies. These are the steps in seven steps.
1.Take care of yourself.
Increasing your education, knowledge, and necessary professional abilities will help you progress in your career. Understanding finance is also necessary to make a living. Additionally, living a healthy lifestyle and being in good health will free up more time for you to pursue opportunities for earning money.

2. Profit from your passions.
You'll be happier, persevere longer, and be more ready to learn more if you can make a living doing what you enjoy.

3. Make spending and savings plans.
It's essential to keep frequent cost records. Your spending habits will be tracked and used for future financial planning. The amount that goes on housing, utilities, food, and transportation—the essentials of life—should not exceed 50% of one's monthly salary. A minimum of 10–20% of each month should be allocated to savings and emergencies in budgeting. Finally, other spending should not exceed 30% of earnings.

4. Spend prudently
It is not necessary to spend more just because you make more money, especially not on ostentatious or excessively opulent items. To become financially independent even sooner, you should invest and save any excess money you have.

5. Establish an emergency fund.
Any time can be a bad time for illnesses, accidents, and the economy. Setting up money for an emergency is essential. A six- to twelve-month fund should be established. Additionally advised are health and accident insurance, which will protect your finances in the event of unforeseen circumstances. At that point, you can live comfortably and stop bothering those who are close.

6. Clear your debts
Credit card and personal loans that have high interest rates should be repaid as soon as possible in order to

avoid taking on more debt of this nature. Furthermore, there should be as little non-performing debt as possible. Once debts are paid off, make an effort to practice greater financial discipline. You must first establish a monthly spending cap, after which you must set aside the necessary funds for savings and monthly expenses.

7. Make retirement plans.

It might be too far for some people to plan. However, you might become financially independent sooner if you start saving for retirement early. This is due to the fact that profits and savings can be amassed and continually reinvested over an extended period of time. It is advised that office workers contribute as much to their company's provident fund as is permitted. If relocating to a new Companies, for your own best interests, it is preferable to move this money with you rather than take it out prior to retirement. Since pension insurance will ensure that you receive a monthly fixed income after retirement, it's also an intriguing retirement savings option. You also qualify for a personal income tax deduction.

Chapter Four; Improved Capability to Make Decisions.

Apply the knowledge you've gained from the past to enhance your decision-making. You can use the decisions you've made in the past to inform your current thinking. To help you make a new, relevant decision, consider evaluating a previous decision and its results.

A useful ability in any workplace is the ability to make effective decisions. Choosing wisely can help you become a more efficient worker, as it can save you time and improve the way you use resources.

How to become a better decision-maker

The following are some strategies to help you become a better decision-maker:

1. Develop a plan.

Making a strategy can be beneficial if you know you will soon need to make a decision. For instance, consider your team's size and individual aspirations in order to determine the most effective way to reach the company's sales target. You can also look into what tools and resources could be able to assist you and your group in reaching the objective.

2. Act Confidently.Attempt to assume control of the decision- making procedure. To guarantee a nippy and effective conclusion, you may try giving the group advice on the advantages and disadvantages of each option and exacting deadlines. This can ease quicker decision-making and boost productivity in a cooperative setting. Another way to hone your strategy chops is to lead the group's decision- making by outlining your favored options.

3. Consult a professional.
You can feel more confident in your decision-making skills and have your decisions validated by getting a second opinion. As always, you can always ask a reliable friend or attempt to find out from a local specialist. To get their perspective on the project you're working on, for instance, you might ask a supervisor.

4. Maintain your perspective.
Consider evaluating each choice's worth. Consider more important choices, like the printing schedule for your organization, rather than wasting time on minutiae like the font choice for your company's literature. You can learn to be more adaptable and capable of making compromises by keeping each decision in perspective.

5. Establish due dates.
Give yourself time constraints for every choice you make. This can reduce the amount of time you have to decide or alter your opinion. It may be necessary for you to first ascertain the significance of your choice. You may need more time to make a decision if it could have a significant impact, which can help you become more adept at time management.

6. Restrict options.
Your decision-making process becomes more complex the more options you have. Reducing the number of options available to you can help you focus on just a few at a time and make better-informed decisions. Restricting your alternatives may also teach you to apply critical thinking to

the remaining ones. For instance, when selecting a photo for your business's social media page, eliminate any that require the visitor to think about it and instead concentrate on photographs that succinctly convey your brand's message.

7. Examine your choices.

Consider enumerating all the advantages and disadvantages of each option. This will enable you to consider all of your options and decisions with knowledge. It might even assist you in coming up with other things to ponder about. Making a list will enable you to consider all the pros and cons of your choice rationally and in an organized manner. You can develop your analytical, critical thinking, and problem-solving abilities by doing this.

8. Work out.

Because it increases energy and stimulates the brain, exercise can help your body and mind function more harmoniously. It may also assist in sharpening your decision-making concentration.

9. Get enough sleep.

Choose the one that is easiest or most comfortable for you when you're weary. We refer to this as decision fatigue. Whenever you can, try to obtain a good night's sleep and use your judgment when making important decisions. If you are unable to do so, take a 30-minute mental break and then revisit the choice.

10. Make new friends.

Having a diverse group of contacts might help you see things from many angles or provide insightful guidance while making decisions. Your collaboration and active listening abilities can be enhanced by collaborating with new friends and coworkers. For instance, you could consult your colleagues on how to tackle a certain project issue. While some people might not have experienced that issue, others might have. You have more people to turn to when you need assistance or reliable counsel if you have more friends and acquaintances.

11. Conduct experiments.

You can use experiments to test your conclusions using mathematical models. If you are uncertain about a conclusion or course of action, you could consider designing an experiment that is comparable to the choice you must make to see what might occur. You can create your experiment protocols by using strategy and research to establish a hypothesis.

12. Acquire and enhance.

Apply the knowledge you've gained from the past to enhance your decision-making. You can use the decisions you've made in the past to inform your current thinking. To help you make a new, relevant decision, consider evaluating a previous decision and its results.

13. Have a rest.

Occasionally, taking a brief pause can assist you in refocusing. Consider taking a quick rest, engaging in some hobbies, or reading a book. You might see your choice from a different angle if you shift your attention to another work.

14. Review the list.

Setting priorities for your decisions may help you become a better time manager and decision-maker. List the things you need to do or decide on, beginning with the most straightforward one. Getting through the list can boost your confidence in your ability to make decisions by giving you a sense of empowerment and accomplishment.

15. Practicing decision-making.

Making decisions frequently can help you hone your decision-making skills in the real world. You may try practicing making basic decisions, like choosing between printing a report in black ink or color. Try practicing making some larger decisions, like which company to purchase a copy machine from, after you feel comfortable making smaller ones.

A common reason why leaders put off making decisions is their intense dread of making a mistake or, worse, of not being liked. But one element should define how much work you might put into any given aspect of the decision-making process: risk. You'll know whether to be more or less careful based on how much risk you assess.

Chapter Five; Better Communication And Relationship Skills.

Transferring information from one location to another is the definition of communication. Communication in partnerships enables you to share with another person your wants and the experiences you are having. In addition to helping you get what you need, communication keeps you linked to the other person in a relationship.

How much communication do we have? nearly the entire time. We conduct phone calls, write emails, attend meetings, compile reports, make presentations, and so forth. Effective communication is a vital component of any successful partnership and a significant aspect of all partnerships. Every relationship has ups and downs, but managing conflict and developing a better, more enduring partnership can be made simpler with a positive communication style.

While we frequently hear about the importance of communication, we may not always understand what it is or how to use it effectively.

In order to deliver powerful, unambiguous messages regarding strategy, customer service, and branding, communication is crucial in business. A company establishing a brand conveys a message that is consistent and suited to its target market. Establishing a good rapport between managers and staff through internal communication promotes cooperation and teamwork.

Others can be captivated, inspired, and motivated by your words. The other person will understand and retain the meaning of your message if you can convey your ideas succinctly and clearly.

It happens to us frequently that we know exactly what we want to say, but the idea gets lost in the translation. This holds true even while we are listening to someone talk. We end up not paying attention because we are lost in our own thoughts.

Speaking effectively is just one aspect of basic interpersonal communication skills. Equally important are your writing style, reading comprehension, and listening comprehension. There's more than one way to communicate your goals.

Speaking can affect everything: tone, pitch, body language, and word choice. For instance, you have to speak in a polite and kind manner with your coworkers. Speaking is more than just using words. When adding intonation and stressors, exercise caution. For instance, when you emphasize something or ask a question, you will use a different tone. You can communicate your meaning and intention clearly and without leaving any room for doubt by learning to speak effectively.

You can be required to write every day at work. Reports, meeting minutes, or notes for your coworkers may fall into this category. Going through pages and pages of writing at work is difficult. Important concepts should always be included at the outset of any communication. You can write more concisely and without needing to include as many explanations if you work on improving your writing skills.

This will not only save time, but it will also clarify your goal immediately.

Paying attention

Despite its apparent ease of learning, listening is one of the hardest skills to master. A dialogue between two or more parties is what communication is all about. Giving people the time and space to express their thoughts is essential to being a good communicator. Take time to consider what they said and pay close attention if they have something to say. Make a conscious effort to listen, rather than just to hear. Ask away if you have any questions. It'll demonstrate your sincere attention.

Perusing

It's not necessary to read a lot of dense books in one night. However, you ought to be able to read crucial work-related documents as well as intricate business reports. It takes more than just skimming the text to determine the author's intent; you must also read between the lines. Having a good reading habit will help you stay organized, even if you have too much to read at work.

Everybody strives to be the greatest at what they do in our competitive world. In order to stand out from the crowd, you must develop your personal brand.

Chapter Six; Increased Self-Respect And Self-Assurance

Put yourself to the test.

Healthy self-esteem, however, does not allow these emotions to prevent a person from attempting new things or accepting difficulties. Establish a goal for yourself, like attending a social event or signing up for an exercise class. Reaching your objectives will contribute to a boost in your self-esteem.

Everybody has moments when they are self-conscious and lack confidence.

However, poor self-esteem can negatively impact our daily lives and mental health if it persists for an extended period of time.

The view we have of ourselves is known as self-esteem.

Positive attitudes about ourselves and life in general are typical when we have a good sense of self-worth. We can handle life's ups and downs better as a result.

A low sense of self-worth often results in a more critical and negative perspective on both ourselves and our lives. Additionally, we believe that we are less capable of overcoming the obstacles in life.

A lack of self-worth frequently starts in childhood. We receive signals about ourselves from our parents, teachers, friends, siblings, and even the media, which can be both positive and negative.

The belief that you are unworthy persists in your mind for an unknown reason.

It could have been challenging for you to meet your own or other people's expectations of yourself.

Stress and challenging life circumstances, including a major sickness or a death in the family, can be detrimental to one's sense of self.

Personality may also come into play. Some people simply have a tendency to think negatively more than others, and some people have unrealistic expectations of themselves.

How does having poor self-worth impact us?

If you lack confidence or self-worth, you can withdraw from social interactions, give up on trying new things, and steer clear of difficult situations.

Avoiding demanding and stressful situations may temporarily give you a sense of security.

Long-term, this can backfire since it feeds your concerns and doubts that are already there. It instills in you the harmful belief that avoiding situations is the only effective coping mechanism.

Having poor self-esteem can negatively impact your mental well-being and result in issues like anxiety and despair.

You can also turn to unhealthy coping mechanisms like binge drinking or smoking.

Ways to take care of your self-esteem
You must recognize and then confront
the self-defeating beliefs you hold in
order to improve your sense of self-
worth.

For example, you can convince
yourself that "nobody cares" about you
or that you're "too stupid" to apply for
a new job.

Start jotting down these pessimistic
ideas and recording them in a journal
or on paper. When did you initially
begin to have these thoughts?

Write some proof to refute these
unfavorable assumptions after that.
For example, "I'm really good at
cryptic crosswords" or "My sister calls
for a chat every week" are examples
of evidence.

Other positive attributes about oneself,
including "I'm thoughtful," "I'm a great
cook," or "I'm someone others trust,"
should be written down.

Include a few positive remarks made
about you by others in your writing.
It's possible that your upbringing has
left you feeling insecure now, but
people may change how they view
themselves at any age.

Chapter Seven; Social and Cultural Influence on the Millionaire Mindset.

Influences from society and culture
are crucial in forming the millionaire
mindset. These variables can affect a
person's perspective and method of

generating wealth in both positive and negative ways.

The social circles and environments in which people interact and grow up play a significant role in shaping the billionaire mindset. Individuals are more likely to develop a similar mindset if they are around people who have a strong work ethic, an entrepreneurial spirit, and financial success. Families that have fostered a culture of wealth creation through the generational transfer of entrepreneurial attitudes and abilities may attest to this.

Cultural factors are also very important in forming the mindset of a millionaire. People may be deterred from pursuing entrepreneurial enterprises by a significant cultural focus on traditional occupations and job security. An attitude of wealth creation, however, may be ingrained in other societies where taking risks and appreciating financial accomplishment are cultural norms.

The millionaire mindset is significantly influenced by the media and popular culture. News reports, movies, and television programs frequently present affluent people as attractive, powerful, and successful. This image has the potential to instill a desire for money as well as the notion that success in business brings contentment and happiness. But it can also breed irrational expectations, pushing people to pursue money without taking into account the underlying dedication and hard work required for success.

Social and cultural factors can also mold a person's perspective on money, achievement, and taking chances. A negative perspective on money accumulation might result from certain cultures' perceptions of prosperity as an indication of immorality or greed. However, societies that value wealth creation and entrepreneurship can also help people adopt an optimistic outlook, be willing to take chances, and strive for financial success.

In general, the millionaire mindset is greatly influenced by social and cultural factors. These factors have the power to mold a person's attitudes, values, and beliefs about entrepreneurship, wealth accumulation, and taking risks. For those looking to develop a billionaire mindset and succeed financially, it may be crucial to comprehend and resist these influences.

Chapter Eight; Maintaining Personal Ethics, Values, and Happiness While Adopting A Millionaire 's Mentality

A well-rounded and meaningful life depends on embracing a millionaire's mindset while upholding one's morals, values, and happiness. Although

pursuing success and money is not intrinsically immoral, it is important to match these objectives with one's moral standards and basic beliefs. Here are some strategies for upholding one's morals, principles, and happiness during the process:
Establish your values and rank them: Take some time to consider what matters most to you and what your basic values are. These could be family, community service, honesty, integrity, or compassion. Make sure your activities are consistent with these principles and that your quest for financial gain does not deviate from them.
Set moral limits: Decide what behavior is appropriate and inappropriate for yourself and set clear boundaries. Establish the moral boundaries that, in spite of possible financial gain, you are hesitant to violate. This could entail abstaining from immoral behavior, lying, or taking advantage of other people.
Make thoughtful decisions: As you go down the route to financial success, keep your eyes on the consequences of your decisions. Think about how it might affect other people, the environment, and your own relationships. You can make choices that support your long-term happiness and are consistent with your values by practicing mindfulness.
Build genuine connections: Assemble a close-knit circle of people who hold similar values to your own and cultivate genuine connections built on mutual respect and trust. Refrain from

forming relationships with people purely on the basis of their financial situation, as this could undermine one's morals or ethical principles. Contribute to society and give back: Accept the idea of helping causes that share your ideals or giving back to your community. Helping others and practicing philanthropy can provide a sense of fulfillment, purpose, and happiness that goes beyond material prosperity.

Strive for financial success while balancing material objectives with personal development: Prioritize personal development, self-improvement, and pursuing worthwhile experiences in addition to financial achievement. Investing in your relationships, personal growth, and general well-being will help you create a well-rounded satisfaction that may endure longer than material items alone.

Develop an attitude of gratitude. Long-lasting happiness can be achieved by showing appreciation for both minor and major accomplishments, as well as for what you already have. Having gratitude keeps things in perspective and keeps you from being obsessed with accumulating wealth.

Recall that assuming the mindset of a millionaire does not mean sacrificing one's morals, ethics, or happiness. It is possible to live a life of integrity, fulfillment, and prosperity by focusing on holistic growth and coordinating your goals with your basic beliefs.

Chapter Nine; The Role Of Self-Discipline And Goal-Setting In Cultivating A Millionaire Mindset.

Developing a millionaire mindset requires self-control and goal-setting. They are crucial elements that prosperous people utilize to meet their monetary objectives and find lasting success.

The capacity to restrain one's impulses, feelings, and actions in order to achieve a particular goal is known as self-discipline. It entails continuously making decisions that support long-term objectives, despite temptations or obstacles that may appear in the short term. Developing a millionaire mindset requires self-discipline because it helps people stay focused on their financial objectives and be willing to make the necessary sacrifices to get there.

People who possess self-discipline are able to withstand the temptation of instant gratification and instead devote their time, energy, and money to pursuits that result in long-term wealth. This entails making wise financial choices, such as putting money aside for savings rather than wasting it, staying out of debt, and persistently aiming to increase assets and income.

Establishing goals is just as crucial to developing a millionaire mindset. A person seeking to accumulate wealth in the financial domain can find direction and purpose in having well-defined goals. Establishing SMART goals—specific, measurable, achievable, realistic, and time-bound—allows for improved planning, progress monitoring, and motivation maintenance.

Successful people frequently have both short- and long-term objectives for their earnings, investments, savings, and total financial development. These objectives serve as standards and guidelines that support people in maintaining their accountability, motivation, and focus. People develop the resilience, adaptability, and willpower to overcome challenges and never give up on their pursuit of financial success by periodically evaluating and revising their goals.

Setting goals also aids in the development of practical plans and tactics that people use to get their intended financial results. It enables people to break down large objectives into smaller, more achievable tasks and benchmarks, which lessens their daunting nature and increases their attainable level. A sense of momentum and success that comes from consistently hitting these smaller goals helps people stay motivated as they move closer to their ultimate financial goals.

In conclusion, goal-setting and self-control are necessary for cultivating a millionaire mindset. Self-discipline enables people to make wise financial decisions and withstand temptations in the short term, while goal-setting provides people with a clear route and motivation to work toward their long-term financial ambitions. Establishing self-control and goal-setting as a way of thinking can help lay the foundation for financial success and wealth accumulation.

Chapter Ten; What You Do With Your Business Will Determine Its Future.

The choices and activities you make as a business owner will determine how your company develops in the future. Here are several crucial areas where your decisions can make a big difference:

1. Strategy: Your company's long-term objectives and direction are described in your business strategy. It includes making choices on growth strategies, competitive positioning, target markets, and goods or services. Depending on how well you make strategic decisions based on market research and how well you adjust to changes, your business will either prosper or fail.

2. Innovation: In today's fast-paced corporate environment, embracing and promoting innovation is essential

to remaining relevant and competitive. You can establish your company as a market leader by implementing cutting-edge technologies, developing new goods and services, enhancing existing ones, and keeping a close watch on market developments.

3. Customer Experience: Your ability to engage with your clients and give them a satisfying experience will have a big impact on their loyalty and word-of-mouth recommendations. The success of your firm as a whole will be impacted by putting a high priority on customer satisfaction, making targeted marketing investments, providing excellent customer service, and getting feedback to improve your offers.

4. People Management: The success and sustainability of your company will be directly impacted by how you hire, develop, inspire, and manage your workforce. Your people are a valuable asset. Attracting and keeping brilliant people requires establishing a positive work environment, encouraging a culture of cooperation and ongoing learning, and offering chances for professional growth.

5. Financial Management: Every organization that wants to thrive must practice sound financial management. The key to making sure your company can continue to develop and maintain its financial stability is strategic capital allocation, careful risk management, precise forecasts, and effective budgeting.

6. Marketing and Branding: Your company's exposure and recognition

in the market are determined by how you position and promote it. Sales can be increased, and your company can differentiate itself from the competition by creating a strong brand identity, putting successful marketing tactics into practice, leveraging a variety of digital platforms, and cultivating relationships with partners and customers.

Recall that your company's future depends on your capacity to make wise decisions, adjust to shifting conditions, welcome innovation, and put the needs of both clients and staff first. You can direct your company in the direction of a prosperous and long-lasting future by doing this.

Chapter Eleven; Accept Failure Rather Than Being Fearful of It.

Failure is frequently viewed in our society as something that should be avoided at all costs. We are indoctrinated to dread failure and to pursue achievement and perfection. In actuality, recognizing failure as a normal part of life can be incredibly liberating and can result in unmatched personal development and success. The advantages of accepting failure rather than letting fear stop us will be discussed in this essay.

Resilience grows from acceptance. We develop resilience when we learn to be at ease with the possibility of failing. Failure is no longer an impassable barrier but rather a stepping stone. Accepting failures as important teaching moments gives us the willpower to keep going.

Resilience is essential for cultivating a growth mentality, which sees setbacks as opportunities for growth and development.

Gaining knowledge by making mistakes:

We can gain important lessons from failure that we cannot learn from success alone. Thomas Edison, one of history's greatest inventors, is credited with saying, "I have not failed. I've discovered ten thousand ineffective methods." Edison's unwavering quest to create the light bulb shows that failure is not a signpost but rather a way to hone and enhance our strategy. Accepting failure allows us to try new things, take chances, and find uncharted territory that could result in ground-breaking discoveries.

Developing fortitude and morality:

We can develop resilience and mold our character through failure. Failure forces us to face our shortcomings, grow in humility, and acquire adaptability. Every setback offers a chance for introspection, personal development, and the acquisition of critical life skills like persistence, self-control, and problem-solving abilities. These lessons will become very useful tools for overcoming obstacles in the future.

Getting over the fear of failing:

Fear of failing can be crippling, keeping us from going for our goals and ambitions. By accepting failure, we face this fear head-on and progressively lessen its hold over us. By embracing failure as a necessary part of the process, we may push ourselves to take chances and go outside of our comfort zones, which creates new opportunities. Our ability to accept failure and become stronger makes us courageous, which helps us move closer to our objectives.

Gaining success from failure: Paradoxically, a lot of noteworthy achievements have come from setbacks. Several business owners, athletes, and artists have experienced failures prior to excelling in their respective industries. Failure is a humble reminder that success is seldom simple or quick. Our mistakes help us become better versions of ourselves, hone our abilities, and lead us to success in the end.

In summary:

When we embrace failure instead of running away from it, we have the opportunity to discover our actual potential. Failure provides a springboard for success and personal development as a result of the resilience and lessons acquired. We may overcome fear, find new opportunities, and grow into our greatest selves when we accept failure as a necessary part of the path. So let's get over our fear of failing and start along the road to incredible success, creativity, and self-discovery.

Disclaimer;

This nonfiction work is founded on in-depth investigation, firsthand accounts, and professional judgments. Despite my best efforts to guarantee the correctness and consistency of the material supplied, I admit that mistakes can be made by humans and that the subject matter is always changing, thus there may be inadvertent errors or omissions.

This book's material is to provide information, viewpoints, and thoughts on the subject matter covered. It is not meant to replace formal education or training, nor to act as legal guidance or professional advice.

When applying the knowledge in this book to their own unique situation or making any judgments, readers are urged to use caution and good judgment. No liability will be accepted by the author, publisher, or distributors for any direct or indirect harm resulting from the use of the material in this book.

Moreover, the opinions contained in this book are the author's own and may not represent those of any persons or organizations mentioned. It is advised to seek the counsel of specialists, professionals, or specialized resources for situation-specific recommendations and individualized assistance.

Finally, to preserve the privacy of those involved, all names, characters, and identifying information mentioned in stories or examples in this book are